CHAMPION
SOCCER CLUBS

MANCHESTER UNITED

SOCCER CHAMPIONS

JEFF SAVAGE

LERNER PUBLICATIONS ◆ MINNEAPOLIS

Lerner Publications Company
A division of Lerner Publishing Group, Inc.
241 First Avenue North
Minneapolis, MN 55401 USA

For reading levels and more information, look up this title at www.lernerbooks.com.

Main body text set in Adrianna Regular.
Typeface provided by Chank.

Library of Congress Cataloging-in-Publication Data

Names: Savage, Jeff, 1961– author.
Title: Manchester United : soccer champions / written by Jeff Savage.
Description: Minneapolis, Minnesota : Lerner Publications, [2018] | Series:
    Champion Soccer Clubs | Includes bibliographical references and index. |
    Audience: Ages: 6–9. | Audience: Grades: K to Grade 3.
Identifiers: LCCN 2017036945 (print) | LCCN 2017039878 (ebook) |
    ISBN 9781541525511 (eb pdf) | ISBN 9781541519879 (library binding : alk.
    paper)
Subjects: LCSH: Manchester United (Soccer team)—History. | Manchester
    United (Soccer team)—Miscellanea.
Classification: LCC GV943.6.M3 (ebook) | LCC GV943.6.M3 S3 2018 (print) |
    DDC 796.334/640942733—dc23

LC record available at https://lccn.loc.gov/2017036945

Manufactured in the United States of America
1-44323-34569-11/21/2017

CONTENTS

INTRODUCTION
THE RED DEVILS

The Manchester United Red Devils were in control. They kept the ball deep in Chelsea's end of the field. Suddenly, United's Jesse Lingard passed the ball to Marcus Rashford. Rashford kicked a low shot from the edge of the **penalty area**, but the ball skipped just wide of the goal. The crowd at Old Trafford stadium in Manchester, England, groaned.

Marcus Rashford was born on Halloween in 1997. It's a fitting birthday for a Red Devil.

Fans can see Red Devils on the field and in the stands at Manchester United games.

Moments later, Rashford had another chance. This time, the **striker** blasted it into the bottom corner of the net. Goal!

The score set off a wild celebration. The stadium shook as more than 75,000 fans jumped up and screamed. Many wore red to match their United heroes.

In England's **Premier League**, the Chelsea Blues were at the top of the standings. The Red Devils were in fifth place with only a few weeks left in the 2016–2017 season. United hadn't beaten the Blues in five years.

Ander Herrera's goal deflected off a Chelsea player before sailing into the net.

United struck again in the second half. Team captain Ashley Young was surrounded by Chelsea defenders. He tapped the ball to Ander Herrera, who drilled a shot into the goal.

Manchester fans chanted, sang, and cheered as time ran out on Chelsea. The game ended 2–0. "Full credit to the fans," said United player Jesse Lingard. "They got behind us all game and created a brilliant atmosphere."

Ander Herrera (*left*) is best known for his defense. His goal against Chelsea was his only score of the season.

1 BUILDING A WINNER

In 1878, railroad workers in Manchester formed a soccer team. The workers called their team Newton Heath LYR Football Club. Most people who live outside the United States call soccer "football."

Newton Heath played against other teams around the city. The players were eager, but the team ran out of money. Then businessman John Henry

Davies bought Newton Heath in 1902. He renamed it Manchester United Football Club.

In 1909, United won England's prized **Football Association (FA) Cup**. Thousands of fans lined Manchester's streets for a parade to celebrate. Old Trafford stadium became the club's home a year later.

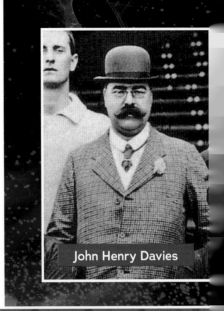

John Henry Davies

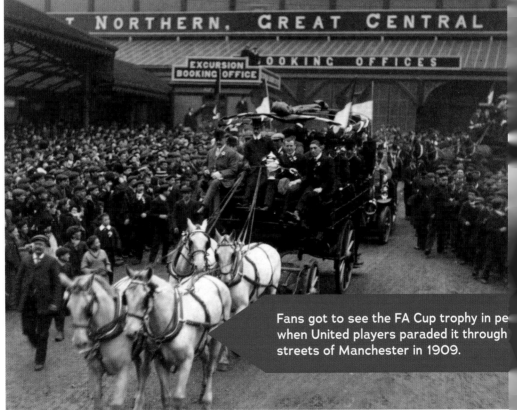

Fans got to see the FA Cup trophy in pe[rson] when United players paraded it throug[h] streets of Manchester in 1909.

The team switched to all-red jerseys in the early 1900s. Color was later added to this black-and-white photo.

World War I (1914–1918) and World War II (1939–1945) disrupted soccer in Europe. Old Trafford stadium was bombed by German airplanes in 1941. United played its "home" games at another team's stadium for several years while Old Trafford was being rebuilt.

United returned to glory thanks to one man—Matt Busby. He became the team's manager in 1945. Busby brought in new players and an attacking style of play. United won the FA Cup in 1948 for the first time since 1909.

In the 1950s, Busby added younger players to the team. Among the new youngsters was 16-year-old

Duncan Edwards. He joined United in 1953 as the youngest player in team history. Busby later called Edwards "the most complete footballer in Britain, possibly the world."

The young group became known as the Busby Babes. In 1956, they beat Anderlecht of Belgium 10–0. It's the biggest margin of victory in United history.

Busby had made Manchester United a power in Europe. But then tragedy struck. On February 6, 1958, the team's airplane crashed during takeoff in Munich, Germany. The accident killed 23 passengers. Among the dead were eight players, including Duncan Edwards.

A combination of snowy weather and engine problems caused United's airplane crash in 1958.

2 DYNASTY

It took several years for United to recover from the plane crash. Matt Busby rebuilt the team. He also gave United the nickname Red Devils around this time. He thought it sounded scarier than the Busby Babes.

The Red Devils won the 1963 FA Cup. United was back on top of English soccer. In 1966, United players

Bobby Charlton, Nobby Stiles, and John Connelly helped England win its only **World Cup**.

United's biggest prize yet came in the 1968 **European Cup** tournament. They faced Benfica of Portugal in the final match. The Red Devils scored three goals in **extra time** to win. They became the first team from England to win the European Cup.

Busby had turned Manchester United into a winner. He retired in 1969, and the team struggled without him. In 1986, the club hired Alex Ferguson

Alex Ferguson coached soccer teams in Scotland before becoming United's manager.

England's top league became known as the Premier League in 1992–1993. Since then, Manchester United have won the league title 13 times. No other team has won the Premier League more than five times.

as manager. Ferguson slowly brought United back to greatness.

In 1993, United won the Premier League for the first time in 26 years. The win marked the beginning of an incredible run of success. They won the league title in eight of the next 11 seasons.

United pulled off an incredible feat in 1999. The team won the Premier League and FA Cup titles. If they could win the **Champions League**, they would capture the rare **treble**.

United trailed Bayern Munich, 1–0, when regular time ended in the final match of the 1999 Champions League. Three minutes of **injury time** were all that remained.

United's David Beckham took a **corner kick**. He sent the ball streaking toward the goal, and Teddy Sheringham kicked it in for the tie. Moments later, Beckham booted another corner kick. This time, Ole Gunnar Solskjaer drilled it into the net. The Red Devils won the Champions League and the treble.

In 2008, United won their third Champions League. The team's 20th Premier League title set an all-time record in 2013. Manchester United has been so good for so long due to one main reason: they've had a lot of incredible players.

United players show off the Champions League trophy in 2008. The silver trophy weighs more than 16 pounds (7.3 kg).

United players celebrate winning the Premier League in 2013. Alex Ferguson retired as manager after the match.

UNITED TIMELINE

1878 Railway workers form the Newton Heath LYR Football Club.

1902 The team changes its name to Manchester United Football Club.

1945 Matt Busby becomes the United manager.

1958 A plane crash in Germany kills eight United players.

1968 United becomes the first English team to win the European Cup.

1999 United wins the treble.

2013 United sets a record with their 20th English league title.

2016 United hires Jose Mourinho to be their next manager.

3 WORLD LEADERS

Manchester United might be the world's most popular soccer team. They have such global appeal that the team's official website can be viewed in seven languages.

A few other big-time teams may rival the Red Devils in popularity. But there's no denying that United is the world's most valuable soccer club. In 2017, it was worth an estimated $3.69 billion.

Fans know Manchester United by many names: the Red Army, the Red Devils or, simply, United. Opponents know them as the enemy. United's success has made other teams take aim at the players in red. Liverpool and Leeds are longtime rivals. Teams such as Arsenal and Chelsea have stepped up in recent years. But United's fiercest rival is also their nearest—Manchester City.

SIDELINE REPORT

During the 2015–2016 season, Manchester United earned $765 million through things like ticket sales and TV rights. That was more than any other soccer team in the world.

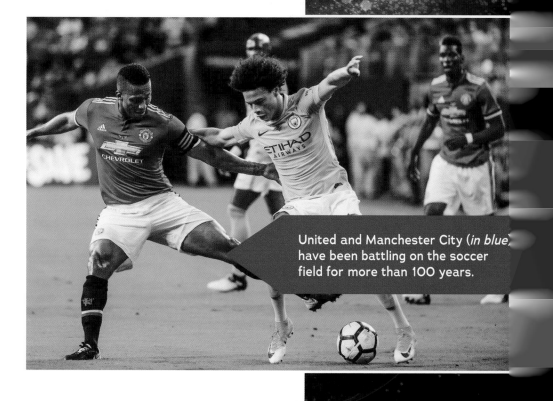

United and Manchester City (*in blue*) have been battling on the soccer field for more than 100 years.

United fans pack Old Trafford to support their club no matter what team they're facing. The crowd chants and sings together as Fred the Red, the United mascot, dances on the sideline.

Alex Ferguson managed United for 27 years. The team never finished below third place in the Premier League with Ferguson as the boss. But in each season since his retirement in 2013, United has finished outside of the top three.

The club may have found its next great leader in

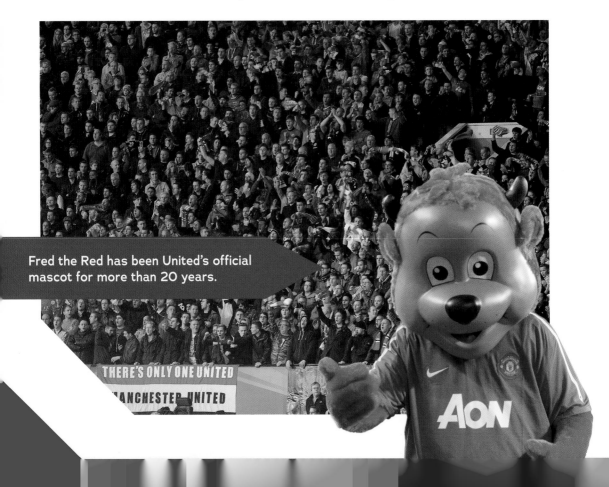

Fred the Red has been United's official mascot for more than 20 years.

THERE'S ONLY ONE UNITED

MANCHESTER UNITED

United coach Jose Mourinho (*center*) has been named the Premier League Manager of the Season three times.

2016. The team hired Jose Mourinho, one of the most successful managers in Europe. Mourinho is thrilled to lead the team. He said United has a "romance about it which no other club can match." Mourinho and his players in red are ready to make sure United stays unmatched on the field too.

4 MANCHESTER UNITED

SUPER

STARS

In 2018, Manchester United fans celebrated the team's 140th season. In that time, superstar soccer players have come and gone from the roster. Read on to learn about some of the greatest Red Devils of all time.

BILLY MEREDITH (1906–1921)

In 1905, Billy Meredith was suspended from the Manchester City soccer team. He had tried to bribe a player on an opposing team. He joined United and helped the Red Devils win two league titles and the FA Cup. He was best known for his long, twisting runs and sharp passes. He usually played with a toothpick between his lips.

BOBBY CHARLTON (1956–1973)

United fans know Bobby Charlton as the team's first superstar. He dazzled defenses as a member of the Busby Babes. Charlton could play any position on the field. His 249 goals were the most in team history until Wayne Rooney passed him in 2017.

Charlton was on board the team airplane that crashed in Germany in 1958. He remembers a loud noise and then nothing. He awoke moments later on the snowy ground, still strapped to his seat. His injuries were minor.

GEORGE BEST [1963–1974]

George Best was probably the finest United dribbler ever. He could twist and turn with the ball seemingly glued to his foot. He once scored six goals in a match. His score in extra time at the 1968 European Cup final gave his team the win. Many fans think of Brazilian superstar Pelé as the top soccer player ever. But even Pelé once called Best the "greatest player in the world."

RYAN GIGGS [1990–2014]

Some fans and sportswriters have called Ryan Giggs the best overall player in United history. He played in 963 games for the team over 23 seasons and scored 168 goals. He helped United win just about every European soccer trophy, including 13 Premier League titles and two Champions League crowns. He became the team's assistant manager when his playing days were over.

DAVID BECKHAM [1992–2003]

David Beckham married a British pop star and was one of the most photographed people in the world. This celebrity athlete was best known for his long-distance passes and pinpoint **free kicks**. His time with United was one of the team's most successful periods. But he was just warming up. After leaving the Red Devils, Beckham went on to win league titles in Spain, France, and the United States.

PAUL SCHOLES [1994–2011, 2012–2013]

Paul Scholes might have been the best passer in United history. He helped the club win 10 Premier League titles before he retired in 2011. A year later, he was back. He came out of retirement to lead the squad to another league title. Then he retired again, this time for good.

CRISTIANO RONALDO (2003–2009)

Cristiano Ronaldo is more than just a soccer superstar. He's an international sports legend and earns more money than any other athlete in the world. He began his career with United and scored 100 goals in his first five years. United shocked fans when they agreed to transfer Ronaldo to another team in 2009. Spain's Real Madrid paid United more than $130 million for Ronaldo.

WAYNE ROONEY (2004–2017)

Wayne Rooney appeared in his first international match when he was 17 and is the youngest player to score for England's national team. He recorded a **hat trick** in his first game for United, and he hasn't slowed down since then. In 2017, Rooney netted his 250th goal to set the all-time United record. He passed legend Bobby Charlton for the honor. "[Rooney] is a true great for club and country," Charlton said.

STATS STORY

Manchester United has dominated English soccer for more than a century. Over the years, the team has achieved some pretty incredible feats. Take a look at a few of the club's most impressive statistics:

PREMIER LEAGUE TITLES: 13

PREMIER LEAGUE MATCHES PLAYED: 1,034

PREMIER LEAGUE WINS: 651

PREMIER LEAGUE GOALS: 1,993

FA CUP TITLES: 12

CHAMPIONS LEAGUE TITLES: 3

MOST GAMES PLAYED: RYAN GIGGS, 963

MOST CAREER GOALS: WAYNE ROONEY, 253

SOURCE NOTES

6   "Match Blog: United 2 Chelsea 0," Manchester United, accessed August 9, 2017, http://www.manutd.com/en/MatchTrackerSeasons/201617/Match -blogs/Premier-League/Manchester-United-v-Chelsea-Premier-League-live -blog-16-April-2017.aspx?AL.

11 Mathias Ask, "Ranking Ryan Giggs against Other Manchester United Greats," *Bleacher Report*, February 18, 2013, http://bleacherreport.com /articles/1533745-ranking-ryan-giggs-against-other-manchester-united -greats.

21 "Serial Winner Jose Mourinho Officially Hired by Manchester United," *USA Today*, May 27, 2016, https://www.usatoday.com/story/sports/soccer /2016/05/27/man-united-hires-mourinho-as-manager-on-3-year-deal /85023210.

25 Chris Murphy, "George Best: Soccer's Ultimate Playboy?," *CNN*, last modified November 25, 2015, http://www.cnn.com/2015/11/25/football /football-george-best-playboy/index.html.

27 Adam Bostock and Adam Higgins, "Record! Rooney Is Reds' All-Time Top Scorer," Manchester United, January 21, 2017, http://www.manutd.com/en /History/Rooney-250/Rooney-250-Goals/2017/Jan/Wayne-Rooney-breaks -Sir-Bobby-Charlton-goalscoring-record-for-Manchester-United.aspx.

GLOSSARY

Champions League: a yearly competition between Europe's top teams

corner kick: a free kick from one of the corners of the field

European Cup: a soccer tournament featuring Europe's top teams. The European Cup became the Champions League in 1992–1993.

extra time: a 30-minute period added to the end of a match when it is tied after regular time

Football Association (FA) Cup: a yearly soccer tournament in London, England, between England's top teams

free kicks: open kicks that a referee awards after a foul

hat trick: three goals scored by one player in a game

injury time: time added to the end of a soccer match to make up for time spent on injuries during the match

penalty area: an area in front of each goal. If a player on the defending team commits a penalty in the area, the other team gets a penalty shot.

Premier League: England's top level of professional soccer

striker: a player whose main job is to score goals. A striker often plays near the opponent's goal.

treble: winning the Premier League, the FA Cup, and the Champions League in the same season

World Cup: a tournament held every four years with national teams from around the world

FURTHER INFORMATION

Braun, Eric. *Incredible Sports Trivia: Fun Facts and Quizzes.* Minneapolis: Lerner Publications, 2018.

Doeden, Matt. *Cristiano Ronaldo.* Minneapolis: Lerner Publications, 2017.

The FA Cup
http://www.thefa.com/competitions/thefacup

Jökulsson, Illugi. *Manchester United: The Biggest and the Best.* New York: Abbeville, 2014.

Manchester United
http://www.manutd.com/Splash-Page.aspx

Premier League
https://www.premierleague.com

INDEX

PHOTO ACKNOWLEDGMENTS

The images in this book are used with the permission of: design elements: Lawkeeper/Shutterstock.com; sakkmesterke/Shutterstock.com; Michal Zduniak/Shutterstock.com; sakkmesterke/Shutterstock.com; somchaij/Shutterstock.com; content: Shaun Botterill/Getty Images, p. 4; John Peters/Manchester United/Getty Images, p. 5; Matthew Ashton—AMA/Getty Images, p. 6; Michael Regan/Getty Images, p. 7; Bob Thomas/Popperfoto/Getty Images, pp. 8, 9 (bottom); EMPICS/PA Images/Getty Images, p. 9 (top); Popperfoto/Getty Images, pp. 10, 11, 12; Bob Thomas Sports Photography/Getty Images, pp. 13, 25 (top); Matthew Ashton/EMPICS/Getty Images, p. 15; Alex Livesey/Getty Images, pp. 16, 18; Tom Flathers/Manchester City FC/Getty Images, p. 19; Martin Rickett/PA Images/Getty Images, p. 20 (top); Nata Sha/Shutterstock.com, p. 20 (bottom); Ververidis Vasilis/Shutterstock.com, p. 21; EFKS/Shutterstock.com, pp. 22–23; Topical Press Agency/Hulton Archive/Getty Images, p. 24 (top); Roger Jackson/Hulton Archive/Getty Images, p. 24 (bottom); almonfoto/Shutterstock.com, p. 25 (bottom); Laurence Griffiths/EMPICS/Getty Images, p. 26 (top); Laurence Griffiths/Getty Images, p. 26 (bottom); LLUIS GENE/AFP/Getty Images, p. 27 (top); Kostas Koutsaftikis/Shutterstock.com, p. 27 (bottom).

Front cover: John Peters/Man Utd/Getty Images; Gareth Copley/Getty Images.